Pra

"Anaphora—the deliberate repetition of a word or phrase—is the major poetic device of Scott Cairns' most recent book of echoes and reiterations tuned to the sound of praise and worship. In other words, Cairns writes to arrive at 'the most of what our words could not.' These poems exalt the lives of his literal forbears—both mother and father—and his poetic forbears, Strand and Stevens. But they manage all this adoration through a real respect for the natural world and the human body as a part of that world, even if that body grows old. Look at what Cairns sees when his eyes do the beholding!"

—JERICHO BROWN, author of *The Tradition: Poems*

"*Anaphora* is a book of both utterance and stillness, written in the language of attention suffused with the sacred. It is a work composed mid-prayer on the threshold of deep encounter, in the liminal spaces of breakwater and tree line, amidst the high peaks of the north Cascades, in forests of cedar and the silence within unceasing longing for God. These are poems of graceful and deft argument, echoing Wallace Stevens, the Book of Psalms, and the homilies of Saint Isaac of Syria, with whom this poet holds particular affinities. Cairns' is a poetry of presence and watchfulness, of elegy and beatitude and counsel on how the just must respond to injustice. It is a poetry awake to love's inspiring agency, soulfully both a burning and a balm, and most especially for our moment, a gift."

—CAROLYN FORCHÉ, poet, memoirist,
author of *The Angel of History* and *What You Have Heard Is True*

"Here is a deft and beautiful collection: poetry as incantation, poetry as both wound and cure. These poems do more than point beyond themselves, for sometimes, in their soft repeated summons, they become the thing they point to."

—MALCOLM GUITE, poet, critic,
author of *Mariner: A Voyage with Samuel Taylor Coleridge*

Anaphora

New Poems

Anaphora

New Poems

Scott Cairns

PARACLETE PRESS
BREWSTER, MASSACHUSETTS

2019 First printing

Anaphora: New Poems

Copyright © 2019 by Scott Cairns

ISBN 978-1-61261-838-8

The Paraclete Press name and logo (dove on cross) are trademarks of
Paraclete Press, Inc.

Library of Congress Cataloging-in-Publication Data
Names: Cairns, Scott, author.
Title: Anaphora : new poems / Scott Cairns.
Description: Brewster, Massachusetts : Paraclete Press, Inc., 2019.
Identifiers: LCCN 2019019058 | ISBN 9781612618388 (tradepaper)
Subjects: LCSH: Christian poetry, American.
Classification: LCC PS3553.A3943 A6 2019 | DDC 811/.54—dc23
LC record available at https://lccn.loc.gov/2019019058

10 9 8 7 6 5 4 3 2 1

Published by Paraclete Press
Brewster, Massachusetts
www.paracletepress.com

Digitally printed

—for Marcia, Elizabeth, Steven, Simon,
Milo, Benjamin, and Kathryn

Contents

II. Other Matter

III. Spare Opacities

IV. Nepsis
[Νήψις]

Preface

For those familiar with literary and rhetorical devices, *anaphora*—the deliberate repetition of a word or phrase—is a familiar strategy, one that both assists textual coherence and draws uncommon attention to the repeated terms. One might recall profound examples of anaphora in biblical poetry and more recently in the Bible-inflected orations of Martin Luther King.

Less familiar, perhaps, is the use of the term in liturgical-Eucharistic settings. Named for the prayer that accompanies the preparation of the Eucharist—a prayer whose structure often employs formal anaphora—the term has come to indicate as well the specific liturgical moment when the elements—the bread and wine—are consecrated, when they become what we in the Eastern Church are pleased to call the Holy Mysteries.

While certain of the poems in this collection employ overt anaphora, many do not. I trust, however, that most will invite a sense of words as doing more than naming, more than serving as arrows pointing to prior substance; I trust that, at least intermittently, these words may acquire due substance of their own, partaking of more than is apparent, the more that is nonetheless *so*, and is present.

Erato at 64

She asked if I still loved her, and I said
       of course, I love you still. I watched to see
if she believed, but all I saw was that
       she wanted very much to so believe.

As for myself, I wanted very much
       to find a word to grant us both assurance,
which is when I saw how words alone would not
       avail, that words alone cannot attain

to evidence, cannot perform a proof.
       I pulled her to the bed. Together, we
addressed the matter of our love, and made
       the most of what our words could not.

I. First Body
[Πρώτον Σῶμα]

Opening the Text

The limen and the choppy line continue
       their provocative confusions at the shore.
The limen and the chattering line obtain a pulse
       as yet absorbing at the shore.
The παραλία, as expected, keeps the sea at bay,
       and we embark from it intent upon what late
familiar measures we might find meet concerning
       how we push our laden coracle once more
into the morning mist. Sublimity proves compelling,
       as a rule, and implicates a matter apprehended,
albeit ever out of view, ever unavailable. Consider it
       as figure for what trembling joy you felt
when, as a child, you stood before the blue Pacific
       and beheld what seemed a pulsing stillness
far beyond the roar, or when you walked
       through low cloud swirling at the ridge, or when
the great elk raised its massive head from undergrowth
       to meet your open eye with his.

Shoring Up and Shoring Down

With near-anaphoric repetition
      the tedious Pacific yet insists
on pressing this our gritty beach
      for further evidence. And look!
At intervals the shore concedes. And Look!
      Here and there the cliffs
reveal the land has altogether
      acquiesced, having shrugged
its shoulders, shedding heaps
      of clay onto the grit.

With near-anaphoric repetition
      the melancholic ebb and flow
repeat their endless question, just as we
      interrogate the rock and clay
and fossil-bearing strata for a clue
      regarding what has brought us here,
regarding what might lead us hence.

Forsaken and Foregone

The ship is slow, and also slow
      the swarthy crew. What's new?

Somewhere far ahead, obscured
      today by low cloud, winter mist,

and, as I say, no small distance,
      the island bides regardless,

and we, ship-bound for the moment,
      have grown a little slow about

our chores, assuming more delays
      in any progress fostering

efficacious effort at the prow.
      What now? You're dozing at the oar.

We're sore, and sorely underwhelmed
      by these our prospects, but admit

it's just that kind of thinking keeps
      the island's promise far away,

unconsidered, unexplored, all
      but impossible to believe.

Conifer Forest
—*January 27, 2018*

More green than blue, more the color
the sea adopts as the sun surrenders to
the western edge, the near, the looming
conifer forest, just now, appears to hang
beneath a tattered shroud, cloud resembling
wood smoke. The resin in the air affords
as well a scent akin to wood smoke hovering.
Many years ago, I walked this very
schist road with my dad—the two of us
with rifles slung, muzzles to the ground,
rifles we were unlikely ever to discharge.
The mist was fresh upon my face, the mist
thinning as we walked. Our *going hunting*
was our way to make a day together, far
from all that might have kept us moving
more apart. As I recall, we hardly spoke,
but savored our slow ascent upon the road,
breathing in the cool obscuring mist, the cedar,
fir, and hemlock. At one point or other, we
found a likely stump atop a clear-cut slope.
We settled there, dropping guns and packs,
sharing coffee from dad's red Thermos cup.
Thirty years ago today, by all appearances,

he left us altogether. In my dreams, he
visits still, walking with me on the schist road,
offering again the sandwich, the steaming cup.

Pemptousia: Πρώτον Σώμα*
—a meditation in the North Cascades, 1976

So I'm wandering along a Cascade trail amid
      gray glacier-melt and shale, attending mostly
to my footing, attending also to a sense of sweet reprieve
      from exile, but recalling even so along the way
the odd term found in Aristotle, a term so often turned
      to *ether*, so often made to serve as just another
glib, essential *element*—deliberate or accidental
      hardly matters—occurring like the other four.

I am recalling also my philosophy class—held
      not all that far from where I wander now—
how the young man who then led our discussion group
      —our professor's hand-picked grad assistant—appeared
so pleased to speak of Aristotle as a man hamstrung by his time,
      as a man thus doomed by his antiquity to see only just
so far. He said of Aristotle once: *embarrassing*, which made
      me as uneasy then as it does now.

Others may have called it *ether*, but Plato's famous student
      seldom did, and when he *did* he meant—I'm guessing—
something more like fire, and surely meant *that* analogically,
      as he was keen to see amid the glitter overhead the traces

of a chance concurrence—both stuff and agency—a likely

occasion, full comprised of matter moved by mind, a prior

body, first dwelling, nearly apprehended, and thus, one gathers,

capable of lending greater substance to our converse here

below.

Meanwhile, here below, I was finding no overt insufficiency,

but found at every turn another vast excess—the great

expanse that was the western slope, its ice and scree just there

above the tree line by a golden sunset lit. And also

—just below the slope where I now choose to stop—a lush abyss

of forest, mist, and swirling light attending the nearly

countless valleys where, for the most part, we yet live and move.

first body, or first dwelling

Adiáphora

Of a misty, low-sky morning pressed
　　　upon the north sound islands there, just
beyond our glassy cove, one might draw
　　　yet another sip from the steaming
cup, and find that, yes, there is so little

　　　to be known, so much to be supposed.

There beyond the concrete breakwater,
　　　the seiner's skiff begins drawing out
the unwieldy net, its tenders all
　　　but indiscernible as they toil
at the stern, even as their modest

　　　vessel skims aloft a gray abyss.

Just now I hear, from crowded branches
　　　overhead the starlings returning
to their habitual questioning.
　　　I, too, resume my late morning mull—
not always the same puzzlements, not

　　　exactly, but, in kind, more or less
approximate. From where I puzzle,
　　　every clarity succumbs again
to appalling generosity.
　　　Each brittle dogma softens in the mist
to far more sympathetic prospect.

Of Late, Our Climate

—*after Stevens*

Behold, ephebe, the sun quakes sinking down
into the cool Pacific's mute sublimity, and calls
to mind the golden peony now coloring
the brilliant bowl of the mind's clear water.
Do you sense the water's trembling? Do you
swoon? The theater has been bereft of late
of any save the tragic character. Consolation
lay, for the moment, in the lovely Labrador
spinning in the sand, even if the beach
recedes, even if the cool Pacific daily swallows
precious ground. Ephebe, the fray is yet approaching.
Do you suppose you are equipped to meet
that storm? The night and all its long-familiar
darkness gathers first behind you, then extends
to fill the vision's scape and scope. The scop
lays down his pen, and leans into the stillness
incrementally absorbing that distance
mistaken heretofore as firm impediment.

Still Life, with Low Cloud and Mist

The cedar weep
      in our green cemetery
where nothing moves
      this morning save
the cedars' shimmering tears.
      The jays have also
stilled their raucous
      song preferring
for the moment
      silently to perch
amid the cedar limbs,
      to blink here mid the mist.
One might think the earth
      itself has of late intuited
good cause for contemplation.
      Such stillness proves
in keeping with
      the heavy drowse
of those beneath the green.

My mother and my father
      sleep beneath one
such ragged cedar.
      On days like this,

we weep together
  with the cedars,
having little left to say.

Inquiry

What was it   trembling
just here   just here
trembling   near the core
the very   base of the heart?
What is it now, still   trembling
within that bright   furnace?
Both a burning   and a balm,
both flame   and flower,
both utterance   and stillness,
the noetic dwelling   has become
since then the welcome   ache, and arc,
both wound   and cure
just here   so near the core.

Appearances

When what the heart most craves, most covets
appears as but some glimmer of the undisclosed
and self-withholding agent, full ensconced behind
our opaque consequences, the moot appearances
are felt to be, in the main, largely disappointing.

You there, with your thumbs poised in familiar
opposition, you may as well relax a bit, and maybe
get a grip. Might it prove enough to observe how all
the pet appearances appear to glare, poised, perhaps,
even to provoke some passing sense of *raison d'être?*

At least, at best, one might yet extend a solicitous hand
to whatever hand yet bides behind the tattered curtain.

Sleepwalking on Water

No boatman, no boat, not much
sense of direction beyond
elsewhere, beyond *I must needs
get me hence*. Late in the day,
I had stepped once more into
the Aegean. I had shed
the day's residue, and was
surprised yet again by how
Aegean saltiness lifts
the body, how easily
I lay upon its waters.
I swam a bit, then rolled
to meet the white Aegean
sky. I must have briefly slept.
And now—some years thereafter—
I startle awake, still held
atop those waters—buoyant,
buoyed, and basking.

Whether awake or asleep,
I do not know.

Glimpses

As when the luminous green
spark of a moment
cries out at the sun's
disappearance over the sea.

As when the salmon's silver
flashes from the sullen green
just off the open bow.

As when at dusk the white
flag of the young doe's tail
sweetens the dimming forest.

As when the infant's flickering
smile mid-nap lifts
the burden of a troubled day.

As when along the mountain path
the low cloud gathers
to cool the pilgrim's face.

As when mid-prayer the icon yet
returns the weary gaze.

Immanence

A Poetry of Ideas
Bereft of its dear body, the airy spirit
      trembles, tossed by every wind.
Bereft of its dear body, the very soul
      swoons puzzling.
Transcendence unattended by dear body
      and its blood proves a dry-
      mouthed, ethereal translation.

A Poetry of Things
As clay left piled on the wheel with no
      fresh animating breath, no hand;
as clay left exposed to all corrosive elements
      with neither shaping nor protecting hand;
so, the referential anecdote denoting
      how very dry the cracker.

Another World in this World
The body rises from its bed, remembering
      how sweet the lover's kiss.
The body rises from its bed, tasting
      of the scented air compounded
      of its own and of the lover's scent.
The body rises to encounter ever
      and again the coupling.

Thanksgivings

Random Beauties

Swallows enlivening the air as the sun descends,
the deep blue coastal range behind which the sun descends,
the varied bands of red and gold across the blue all rising
as the sun descends, and these the dimming eyes beholding.

And Also Crows

Especially in the midst of their return at dusk, their several solo
or well-companioned dipping, rising, all-but-iambic flights
to the somewhere tree invisibly east of here,
where they gather in community to rest; but also those
many who tidy up the shore so often littered with the sad
debris of crabs and clams and mussels, the odd abandoned
crust of bread. I should not fail to mention those several whose
raucous days fill the cedars at the back of our lot, and the
   amicable
few who are pleased to visit more intimately our back porch,
   retrieving
the few bits of kibble that the dogs have left in or near
their shiny bowls, those few who gather scraps and wash them
in the cobalt birdbath at the high and quiet corner
of our uncommonly satisfying realm.

And Yes, Harbor Seals

They seem nearly to attend us as we walk our Labradors along
    the pebble beach;
they seem so nearly Labradors themselves, offering their
    customary open
gaze, their eyes like shining ebony, the bristled mottle of their
    slightly
bobbing faces, and the nod of blessing they bestow before they
    disappear.

II. Other Matter

An Opening

The center of the page insists on being where—
precisely where—the margins meet.

The center of the page avails for any
who would approach it yet an entryway.

Once that port has opened to the eye,
the center of the page obtains

for any who arrives an opening.

Slow Pilgrim

I saw the road, and saw myself, and fled.

Suppose the pilgrim's ready. Let's say
that he begins. Let's say he lifts his bed,
and stuffs it in a sack, then wanders off
into the rain, determined now at least
to make a fitting end. Thus, of one, late,
given day, while cedars weep and hemlocks
dip their crests, the bracken drip and tremble
as a pool of varied green. As he sets off to beat
the underbrush, an indistinct and mute
immensity obtains *en route*. Just so.

Therein, a long-held, dim desire for what
might pass for progress leads him to a road,
and lately to a narrow path inscribed
to cross a wilderness, where, with something
of an unaccustomed turn, that same vague
wish becomes a taste for the vertiginous,
a vast expanse upheld, if not contained,
just here among the bracken as perhaps
within one's own walled garden's hidden grove.
The wish occasions, then, another opening

and momentary glimpse, within which more
than can be gathered is nonetheless beheld.

The City
—after Kavafy

When I arrived at last I said aloud
at last, I have arrived. And I was pleased
to have at long last freed myself from all
the grit and grimy matter of the poor,
regrettable metropolis I'd fled.
It may have been the city of my birth,
but still it felt as if it would become,
for all its charms, the city of my death.

This city, ancient as it was, spread out
before me like a dewy promise kept.
As I passed through the gate I took in all
that lay ahead—the market's spice, its roar,
the colorful array of persons, each
clamoring for coins and brilliant goods.
I hurried in, full willing to be lost
amid the unknown passages I'd sought.

Matter of Translation

Καθώς εργάζονταν το σχήμα,

εργάτης σε υαλουργείο,

κατάλαβε πολύ καλά τον έρωτα

για την ύλη,

όπου φυσούσε την πνοή του.

—Ζωή Καρέλλη (1901–1998, Thessaloniki)

All morning I have mulled, have pored

over both the curious Greek,

the more curious translation.

Of what Zoé Karélli wrote

I dare to shape the following:

As the figure worked,

the worker in glassblazery,

he understood very well the love

for matter,

which blew the breath.

Her late translator, however,

has offered what seems a lovely,

if yet inexact replacement:

> *As he wrought the shape,*
>
> *a worker, a blower of glass,*
>
> *felt his love profoundly*
>
> *for the material*
>
> *into which he blew his breath.*

No lover of Gnostics, I too
share with Kimon Friar the joy
in honoring the matter ever
at hand, but I would say I miss
the subtle gesture our Zoé
has shaped suggesting it is love
proves agent of the shaper's breath,
while all the while the willing
artificer but bears witness
to love's inspiring agency.

Exhumation

—after Zoé Karélli

They made packages of the human presence,
in order—one presumes—to return
whatever remained of him to native land.

I daresay that the clay from which those
sallow bones were drawn just may have proved every
bit as native to their flesh as any clay—

maybe even more so, now that this
young man's flesh had been infused so completely
into its shallow grave. Like the poet whose lines

have hurt me efficaciously, I
will lament, but nonetheless observe how such
beauty bides despite attendant grief,

how this particular beauty must
rise only from the ache of just such deep grief.
From the earth, into the earth, comprised of earth,

all our circular journeys attest
to this most compelling of confusions.

Fabric: Regarding Vesalius

—Whatever this was to them,
it is all yours now.

What matters most is most infused
within the patent matter of the host.
What matters most is often lost
whenever one sees fit to parse *the one*
into a splay of bright constituents.

Observe, just here, the keen degree
to which a honed indifference attains
its edge, and pares away what may
have kept us innocent and sick. The trick
lies yet in severing one's sense of *he*

from him whose glib humanity
proved impediment to excavation
heretofore. We must admire what
special art obtains for us so clear, such
obvious advantage, the price of which

—by all appearances—was one man's soul.

Archaeology: A Late Lecture

Debris and caked accretion keep
the past interred, until one takes
the spade, and makes a start to find
amid the several strata some
encouragement, some clue to how
we've come to be, have come to be
—belatedly—*thus*. As we are
at present also somewhat caked
in varying degrees of grit,
we find with every shovelful
of artifact a mirror now
evincing just how far we have
not come. Every decade falls,
and, therefore, yet, it falls to each
and every one of us to grip
the spade, to put our backs into the dig.

Babel's Artifacts

The construction proved without
conclusion, save that every stone
retained its shape wherever chance
would carry it—chance and mute
confusion, well, chance and mute
confusion, and our increasingly
nattering tribe. The broad museum now
spanning cross the globe remains
the only lasting structure, though
even so, its rooms are dimly lit,
and we, too simply lit, and we,
become too certain of our terms.

The Blesséd Gates of the City

The governors are lately resolute,
to shut for good the heavy gates, the gates
that long have served as open, wide embrace
receiving those whose sufferings elsewhere
have set in motion their late trek toward
new life. The governors have thus obliged
many men in uniform to wrestle closed
the heavy gates, but note, the heavy gates
will not be moved. The citizens therefore
have come out with festive gear and giddy
spirit to watch the doomed attempt to doom
those coming to the gates. The heavy gates
will not be moved. Pray for the now chagrined
men in uniform, that embarrassment
will not lead them into further sin, further
failure to be men with wisdom enough
to refuse the governors when those same
governors forsake the deeper mandate.

Tempest

—1982, Paul Mazursky, director

Kalibanos welcomes you to his comfy cave,
and if the Sony Trinitron proves defective
so too does the illusion that you had slipped free
from the world and its ubiquitous corruptions,
that you could simply say you would no longer play
the soul eroding role of mute, complicit slave.

Many frames will roll revealing what lit form your
future may attain, but the storm will not relent.
You must know that. Evasion serves for a season,
but you will be obliged—even in the midst of
every good intention, every effort at late
reconciliation—to seize the goat, to raise
the knife, to make the necessary sacrifice.

Sweet Life
—La Dolce Vita *by Federico Fellini*

In a frame or two, Marcello
will turn away, finally having
failed to hear her voice, the angelic
girl beckoning from across
the estuary's rift in the beach,
etching in the sand the divide
between his world and her world.

Behind him, in that flat expanse
to which he will soon turn, waits
the monstrous ray, decaying
in the sand amid a gathering crowd
of what would seem the similarly perplexed.

Just before turning, he will raise
his hands, he will shrug, surrendering
all hope of hearing what it is
she means to say to him, her voice
eclipsed by surf, blown elsewhere
by ocean breeze. Still, don't
look at him, witness now the sweet
and—as I say—angelic offering
he can no longer hear.

My Dog and My God

My dog Sophia sits this evening watching me,
attending to my every move. I don't move much.
She has been fed, and walked, and run, and now we sit,
amid my study's clutter, within a sudden
stillness that obtains for us a momentary
meeting of the minds, quite like conversation.

I love my dog, have loved my every dog, each being
his or her own, particular joy, and each,
by proving thus particular, becoming thus
beloved, has offered me a glimpse of how the God
may have deemed me loveable, if very often
disobedient, and very often reeking
of the death in which I've been inclined to roll.

Rose Tear

—sentiments for Georgi Andreev, and all Bulgaria

What tenderness is this? What kiss
so wounds the heart (with beauty?) that the mind
and heart both spin to one delicious swoon,
promising to keep the soul both brave and kind?

What courage blossoms ever from this flower
of the heart? What music rises to embrace
the light now rising in the east, reaching
as enchanting scent to stir a waking strength?

It is the ancient gift of this, your home,
your native soil, the gift of blessèd land.
It is the symbol of your kindred, kept
and passed along by every gracious hand.

This is the oil of your anointing, and sacred vow.
This is the fragrant prayer we offer ever, offer now.

Recurrences

The motif ever as expected
      returns to repeat both the tenor
and the tone. The familiar motif
      strings its ligament and tendon
mid the somewhat denser bone
      supporting shape, and implicating
what might yet rise into view. All
      that's new abides observed
as that from which such motif
      flows, as that to which it leads.
We see in that so-subtle agency
      ourselves as threads drawn through
the several yet discrete occasions
      that comprise some measure more
than our own apparent incoherence.

III. Spare Opacities

Progression, with Cliché

I've been trying *to make myself clear*,
      have been scrubbing away the debris
that insinuates dimming effects
      so completely that I cannot see
so much as an instant ahead.

I've been hoping *to get to the point*
      where my prayer becomes wrapped in my thought,
and that thought becomes, ceaselessly, prayer.
      Still, for all good intentions, the gap
appears yet to widen instead.

I would ask if *it is what it is,*
      this apparently endless chagrin
that accompanies ever my thought
      and my prayer, ask if maybe one day
the nous will yet deign to be whole.

Sleeping Dogs

I cannot help but wonder what they're thinking as
they sleep. Is that a smile? They often seem to smile
in their sleep. I think that I have loved every dog
I have ever met, even Dana, the Great Dane of my belovéd
cousins, who once and uncharacteristically
bit my face as I leaned in to kiss her head when
I was six years old. I do forgive her, of course,
and am pleased to remember how, thereafter, she
covered my face with kisses every time we met.
Forgiveness all around.

                             But back to sleeping dogs.
I wonder what they're thinking—when they smile, or when
they whimper, or when they, for all appearances,
must imagine that they run.

                            In my own dreams, I
have met again my several beloved dogs, have run
with them, embraced them, nuzzled their soft
and sharply wax-scented ears. I suppose that if
anyone were to watch me sleep, she would see me
smiling, running, nuzzling the pillow like a dog.

Says Tina

Green is not your color, says Tina.
You do somewhat better with blue.
I slip off the green jacket for return
to the clearance rack. The solicitous
clerk turns away to confer
with Tina, who surveys the blue jackets.

I probably have plenty of jackets,
but we have a dinner next week, and Tina
says I should *Get something new*. Tina confers
her approval for my buying something blue.
The salesclerk also approves, her solicitous
smile softens store policy *vis-à-vis* returns.

As all sales are final, with no hope of return,
I feel I must examine all available jackets.
Uncharacteristically solicitous
Tina lifts two. *Try these*, says Tina.
Both strike me as likely; both are blue.
I slip on the linen as the women confer.

Tight at the shoulder, it seems to confer
an odd muscularity, so I return
it to Tina, who says *but I adore this blue*,

and I like when you wear less baggy jackets.
I know an imperative when I hear it, and say to Tina,
Sorry, I had no idea. I mean to be solicitous.

The clerk, being nothing if not solicitous,
suggests I try it on again, confers
theatrically—*sotto voce*—with Tina
as I take the jacket and make my return
to the bright, half-circle of mirrors. I have lots of jackets.
It won't hurt to choose Tina's blue.

I say *Yes, it is a very nice blue,*
and I'm not simply being solicitous.
I do have a good many jackets,
and this one, I daresay, confers
a younger áffect, an almost return
to earlier days, back when I first met Tina.

Of all my jackets, this agreeable blue
seems most pleasing to Tina. So, sure, I'm being solicitous.
It confers yet a time to which I'd gladly return.

Spare Opacities
—after Mark Strand

I was talking with my sister about her preference for the denotative poem, which is a preference I cannot share. She was staring out the window, and, far as I could tell, was studying the neighbor's gray cat, which—for its part—was studying our bird feeder, its tail twitching just enough to keep the birds from lighting on the feeder. "I find comfort," she was saying, "in words that point directly to things, words that *mean*." I looked into my cup where the dark sheen of the coffee offered an image of the skylight in miniature. "But Sis, words that serve only to point to prior things have acquiesced to the least and lowest operation of meaning, as well as to the poverty of the nonexistent mean; they are also, I daresay, *mean*." She turned from the window to face me. "You're always doing that, taking a simple, an honest statement and making it so goddam loaded, so goddam ambiguous that it doesn't mean *any*thing. I like poems that point to real things, real events, actual feelings." The coffee had gone a little cold, but its bitterness brought a surprising freshness to the tongue. "That's exactly the problem," I said to her. "The word or poem that points only to appearances can never get anywhere *near* the real, which is necessarily comprised of what is *not* apparent, even as it offers and honors what *is*." She collected her things, getting ready to leave, clearly planning to say nothing more. I couldn't stop talking. "I like when poems help me see things differently, or when I register a faint shock of recognition in their terms." As the door closed behind her, I felt suddenly very sad, and drained my cold cup.

Κοσμοκαλόγερος
—Kosmokalógeros, a monk in the world

Papadiamandis wakes in midnight dark, and he
is pleased to find the prayer already on his lips,
the prayer he has acquired, a work of many years.

Old Papadiamandis blinks there on his pillow, moves
his lips, and in the swirling mottled dark above him sees
the darkness shaping what he takes to be reply.

Some hours hence, he will rise, will make his way
along the narrow hallway to the amber icon corner
where the lambent vigil lamp avails an amber glow,

where rest the several icons of his most belovéd
saints, the Lord, the Holy Mother. He will lean in
to kiss each one as he prepares descent into the heart

to greet again the one who prays there, ever.
This deep, incessant conversation often wakes him
in the dark, and often in the dark he breathes

the prayer, attending to the darkness, the vivid
stillness it affords, and, once more, both in rising up
and falling back, he breathes a seamless prayer.

No text, no map, no paraphrase

can offer what is due to that
    with which the air is thick.

When even what one sees extends
    quite patently beyond the ken,
        one gains a taste for that which spins

forever past appearances,
    beyond what lies here manifest
        with grit and wind-spun element.

Such limit—coupled with an ache
    deep in the throat—is sole poor proof
        of the sublime, its ever more,

its vertiginous expanse. Good chance
    the mind will dim to darkness, still,
        and very good the chances that

what passes for the self will shift
    to yet another register—
        and full unrecognizable.

That said, all *saying* in the mean-time halts
    well shy of comprehension, and well shy
      of what one might even so suspect.

Poem
—homage to Mark Strand

I gaze upon the poem,
duly lined, laid out
upon my plate, and over it
I pore, inhaling
its juices—the carrot
and onion—and something
of the man whose memory
is thereby invoked. Of late
I find I do regret
the passage of time,
its remissions, re-
tractions, dissolutions
of what has been—if
elusively—mine. I pause
in memory's lit moment
before a familiar window facing
down the slope of avenues
and, as in late summer evening
light, upon the rose-stained
brick and wood-frame
bungalows below, and barely
register that I see no
living thing—not a bird,
not a branch in bloom,

not a soul moving in the rooms
behind the darkened panes.
These days when one finds less
and less to love, less to praise, one
could do worse than yield
to the power of past sustenance.
So I bend to inhale steam rising
from my plate, and I think
of the first time I tasted
a roast like this. It was
years ago, in Seabright,
Nova Scotia; my mother leaned
over my dish and filled it,
and, when I finished,
filled it again. I see
the gravy, recall its scent
of garlic and celery, and sopping
it up with pieces of bread.
And now I taste it again.
The meat of memory.
The meat of no change.
I raise my fork in praise.
I take all that has been
given, and I eat.

Which Tribe? Which River?

So, where do you go when memory proves
mostly worthless, when after three generations
of willful neglect you find the road home
nearly impassable? At my father's funeral
an ancient, dark-eyed woman showed up
just long enough to say two things: hello, good-bye.
I was busy staying numb, so never
took the chance to find out who she was.

In Washington State, every river gets a tribe.
Big rivers often get two, one clan for each muddy,
gravel bank. You already know about the rain,
so you might guess about the rivers. Hundreds
draw their waters from the glacial blue, snow melt,
the nearly endless seasons of rain. Turns out,
the woman was my father's kin, turns out my great-
grandmother may have been Nisqually.

Which, presumably, makes me something I never
exactly knew, but had overheard a piece of maybe
once or twice at my own grandmother's house,
when one or another uncle had drunk his fill,
when the family reunion had suddenly become
more colorful. I recall certain liquor-blunted faces,
a slew of slurred obscenities, and that my parents
stuffed me in my coat as we headed for the car.

Well, like I said, the tribes are numerous and famously
intractable, as well as hard to track. So I've unrolled
my father's map, which offers someone else's best
guess at tribal boundaries. And I've dusted off
a lately disinterred family Bible—a very poor edition
with a poorly kept family tree, and—though I know
better than to trust it—I've resorted to memory.

Sin *En Route* to Lent

Beneath his breath
the zealot says
thank God I am
not like this man,
the Pharisee
who thought to scorn
the publican.

Late Sayings

Blessed as well are the wounded but nonetheless kind,
      for they shall observe their own mending.

Blessed are those who shed their every anxious defense,
      for they shall obtain consolation.

Blessed are those whose sympathy throbs as an ache,
      for they shall see the end of suffering.

Blessed are those who do not presume,
      for they shall be surprised at every turn.

Blessed are those who seek the God in secret,
      for they shall know His very breath rising as a pulse.

Blessed moreover are those who refuse to judge,
      for they shall forget their own most grave transgressions.

Blessed are those who watch and pray, who seek and plead,
      for they shall see, and shall be heard.

Which Cup? What Baptism?

Can you drink the cup I drink or be baptized
with the baptism I am baptized with?

—Mark 10:38

As with many disconcerting
                puzzles, as with most
questions one may first be slow

                or too embarrassed to answer,
his provocations can educe

                a glib array of other
questions, most of which

                are offered mostly to defer,
evade, or qualify one's

                shamed reluctance to say yes.

Which cup, Lord? What baptism?

                Who am I to say?

In any case, I daresay Jesus

                is not speaking of the cup
at Canna, nor of that cup

                requested of Photiní;
neither—I'm guessing—

                does he indicate so much
the cup he offered his disciples

                on the night he was betrayed.

The *cup* that he himself

           would have forgone

—had it served

           the Father's will—is far

more likely the bitter

           vessel implicated here.

Nor is his humble dipping

           in the Jordan—so brief

a descent—likely to be

           the *baptism* posed before

two suddenly bold disciples,

           both of whom would

one day—even so—drink,

           descend, and be interred.

In one of *his* most curious

           locutions, Saint Paul

writes that he rejoices

           being called to offer up

with *his own body*

           his share in *what*

is lacking—υστερήματα—

           in the sufferings of Christ,

that he is pleased

           to undertake whatever yet

is to be done.

And what of us, languishing just
                    here, perplexed amid
the puzzlements? What *is*
                    left waiting to be done?
I would suppose that we
                    must surely drink, descend, and drown.

Sermon against a Meddling God

All streams flow into the sea,
yet the sea is never full.
　　　　—*Ecclesiastes, Words of the Gatherer*

Not the *actual* God, Whose Hand
　　　　is exceedingly slow to tweak
　　　　our dimming circumstances, loathe
　　　　to eclipse our willfulness, nor
　　　　so much as trouble the queer
　　　　pertinacities of the herd,
　　　　nor quell our bovine insistence
　　　　that we be left to our odd taste
　　　　for an increasingly bitter cud.

Rather, the dominant fiction
　　　　narrated for centuries by
　　　　whole colleges of sequential
　　　　myopic theologians—*allegéd*
　　　　theologians, I should note,
　　　　who seldom deign to descend
　　　　into so slight a thing as prayer,
　　　　theologians whose illumination
　　　　remains but a trick of light and mirrors,
　　　　whose vision is confined to dim
　　　　aspects there within the mirror.

These have bequeathed to some dozen
       generations the fib that all
       that happens is God's will,
       that we need only learn the script,
       recite on cue, and suffer in blithe
       accordance to His petulant dictate.

Whenever we aver that He
       has taken one of us, each time
       we infer His hand in any
       rending devastation, we both
       blaspheme, and shirk our own
       complicity. The world is ours
       for mucking up, as is every
       fancy we may entertain
       about the God. Any figure
       you might shape as idol in lieu
       of the Inexhaustible is sure
       to prove a heresy against
       the very God Who has occasioned you.

Recreation

And when we had invented death,
    had severed every soul from life
    we made of these our bodies sepulchers.

And as we wandered dying, dim
    among the dying multitudes,
    He acquiesced to be interred in us.

So when He had descended thus
    into our persons and the grave,
    He broke the limits, opening the grip,
    He shaped of every sepulcher a womb.

How, Then?

...πώς να μιλήσεις με τους πεθαμένους*
—*after Seferis*

Following the last syllables of my evening prayers, just
as my evening prayers have ceased, though the very air
remains infused with their improbable fragrance, I raise
the agapanthus near the censer, raise the censer, lift
my thereby stilled heart to speak aloud what it so often
dares utter only in silence. In the hollow there, scoured
of daily chatter, emptied of the day's debris, I dare
to speak intimately with my father and my mother, asking
that they remember me as I remember them, asking that they
also speak as I have done, praying yet for their children
and grandchildren, praying also for our Simon, and for other
blessed offspring to come. How can I comprehend
or so much as *come to terms* with this impossible faith?

*how to speak to the dead

IV. Nepsis

[Νήψις]

My Malady

A crime has occurred, accusing all.
—from Auden's *The Age of Anxiety*

The disease is unpronounceable. The disease is, nonetheless
or therefore, quite incurable, as one cannot address what one
cannot address. I first suspected the extent of my own affliction
of an autumn afternoon in Orvieto. The clouds dispersed
suddenly from above my high perch at the plateau's western
edge, revealing a ruddy-golden light igniting all the thick,
medieval stone, revealing a profound and golden green laving
the valley below San Giovenale where I sat on a wooden bench,
and revealing yet how unshakable my sense of dread. Even the
rich cigar between my knuckles proved powerless against that
deep dismay, as did the chattering martins flitting through the
golden air, as did the resin-scent of cypress. I turned to enter
the empty church. My dread followed close, and sat nearby as I
hunkered into prayer. I observed, regardless, the slow accretion
infiltrating cell by cell, colonizing with its leaden weapons my
beloved person. How might I name this? How recover?

No Remission

When my father died, I slipped
    into a sort of dread
that keeps me staring still
    into a sort of dread.

The cemetery cedars weep
    within low cloud
and we look past the chill,
    into a sort of dread.

This whiskey, iced and held
    within the leaded glass,
can dim my drifting far
    into a sort of dread.

I draw what breath I can
    within the closing air.
That said, still, my best thoughts spill
    into a sort of dread.

For all of that, the day
    is warm and bright.
For all of that, my big dogs all but fly
    across the winter field.

Isaák (pray for him) is slipping still
      into a sort of dread.

Ειρήνη
—poem for my mother

I knew that she was dying. *She*
also knew, had said as much, just
some moments before her final
words to me. The several nurses
stopped by every hour or so
to note my mother's labored
progress. Arvo Pärt's *Alina*
sweetened the room. I gave her yet
another sip of water, smoothed
her cooling brow, and studied her
bright face, her throat's diminished pulse.
When my voice would let me,
I said aloud my only prayer.
Her last words were not addressed to me.
She raised her arms, and made one final
plea, saying harshly *take me home, take me!*

Beyond Knowing

—η ειρήνη του Θεού η υπερέχουσα πάντα νουν*

The peace I hope to know is that strange peace
   surpassing knowledge, that deep peace
one finds most often in the brief descent
   that drops the pilgrim to his knees.

Abandoned at the bottom of the well
   the dear belovéd son might still
uplift his eyes to witness through his tears
   the calm obtaining mid the stars;

in the sea beast's hollow gut, the duly
   chastened prophet might yet extend
his arms accepting the embrace that serves
   to prove a new serenity;

thrown by burning men into the furnace
   the three astonished youths might stand,
refreshed, wrapped in cool vapor, made
   quiet by the presence of another.

the peace of God, supreme, beyond knowing

And here, amid the daily tumult, we
	might still descend into what calm
lies waiting in the bower of the heart,
	a stillness, ever beckoning.

Of the Raven

In the likeness of the Raven, my father carved
a cedar rattle before he died. I keep it
among the other relics of a tribal life which
endures, if faintly, in mists and clouded forests
of a ruined peninsula. Crushed abalone shell
gives the bird its voice—bright, liquid, inhabited.

If you could look inside, witness the brilliant flash
of rainbow shell in sunlight, you would have
an image for that sound—brittle points of flame, cold,
blue, ready to fly. But they are shut away,
unavailable to the eye, known only by a luminous,
dry clatter, and by its haunting claims.

Honor

Honoring my mother, I have christened
my boat Ειρήνη.* Honoring my dad,
I keep a crab pot on the bow, two poles
upright adorning the stern. Here,
afloat, honoring the home my parents
chose to build for me, honoring their gifts,
I drift amid late days meandering
these straits, the ebb and flow of just such salt
passages as they once floated in their day.
Of a given morning, I too set out
among our stone and coarse-sand beaches, pleased
by the swelling Sound, attended by a wash
of vivid memory. I almost see
their bright faces leaning in to bless my
quiet loll among the several islands
hereabouts, where peace is both profound
and ever beckoning of what seems now
an ongoing conversation with them both,
and also with the God who has seen fit
to draw me home to calm these latter days.

*Irini, meaning "peace"

Broken Body Prayer

If I am of the body, of your most
      belovéd body, then I am sorely
severed—both meet and right that I should be

cut off from your otherwise immaculate,
      your otherwise praiseworthy, your most pure
and comely body. If ever I may

have partaken of your endless life as you
      once partook of this my own and patent
death, that vivid pulse has since been quieted

to little beyond an inexpressive
      ache, and I will take that untoward dimming
to suggest a late, most acute parting

from the lifeblood coursing through everything
      that lives and moves, every other thing as well.
I am broken, am most broken. Remember me.

Late Metanoia
—μετάνοια*

As we have all denied him, as we all
have grown more lost along the way, we need
now answer his most simple question: *Do*
you love me?

   Should we deign to answer *yes,*
yes, yes, you know, Lord, that I love you, then
we must rise up, set out to feed his lambs.

As we have all made what little progress
we have made in fits and starts, as we all
have gained some ground, lost most of it again,
the question

   comes around again each day:
How shall I yet hope to love him, how make
of this my love a covert for his sheep?

*to redirect one's nous, the intuitive heart

Premonition on the Holy Mountain
—remembering Brett Foster

In Vatopaidi's dark *katholikón*
the liturgy has just begun, though we
three pilgrims have stood propped in our *stasídi*
for, lo, three dark hours already. The Psalms,
the Midnight Hours, the Matins—all have filled
our drowsy heads with Greek as we have drifted
in and out of what seems very like a dream.
It seems a dance, it seems a slow, a ceaseless
prayer, and, when I close my eyes, I feel
that I am also dancing with a crowd
of silent witnesses. It is a taste—
one might suppose—of what one finds interred:
embraced, asleep, and biding time in peace.

Just now, three tall thin monks float into view
to set lit tapers to the oil lamps,
and we awaken to the call announcing
"Blesséd is the kingdom of the Father,
of the Son, and of the Holy Spirit."
I turn to see my friend. He has fully
wakened now, his face aglow, his face aflame,
his lovely spirit singing *Blesséd is the name.*

Daily Sacrifice

All but unsuspected, the deaths that feed
accrete, surround, and all but swallow up
the pleasures one receives with every bite
of roast lamb set upon the tongue, with each
sweet bit of cod thus borne upon the fork.
The slaughter's indiscrete, but radiates
to compass all our green surround. Each leaf
and every tasty root has likewise fed
on death, the very soil manifesting
every moment one dim microscopic life
surrendering in death its all to yet
another lucky bug, whose luck will soon
 run out to feed the next. A smiling vegan's
chauvinism is complex, but no less
specious than my own. The carrot's death—or
onion's, apple's, fig's—proves likewise no less
sacrifice than the tender lamb's, and we
are no less implicated in the scheme. Eat up.

Interior Asides

Dive into your self, away from sin,
and there you will find the steps
by which you can ascend.
                    —Saint Isaak of Syria

Here along the limen, laden

    with anxiety, a downright

    heavy bag and right unwieldy,

the latter-day *scop* shores up

    his wits with a heady smoke met

    with good malt whisky neat. As most

things go, it's not so bad. The view

    avails a sense somewhat akin

    to vertigo, but that swoon too

becomes becoming as one's dim

    wits acquire a rare density

    sinking to the core where they quell

the rising pulse. Here, have a sip,

    and have yourself a look around.

    If you're in luck the spinning, spare

interior proves every bit

    expansive, inexhaustible

    as the luminous span beyond.

Anaphora on Orcas Island

—after Stevens

To behold the sublime, one must first
      accede that one is also held, beheld,
beholden to. One must first agree.

To behold the sublime, one must first
      forgo one's taste for standing clear,
for standing far apart. One must see.

To behold the sublime, one must first
      suspend the long-held lie of self-
sufficiency, accept the pulse. The sky

—held close to all that lay in view,
      with mist and wood smoke mingling
low amid the deep expanse of green—

availed a glimpse, if momentary,
      of what one's hunger might occasion,
shy of satisfaction, even so.

Anaphora of Basil the Late

O Holy. O Holy Silent Father
    Inexpressive.

O Mother All Compassionate. O Most
    Adorable

and, yea, allegedly, Most Adoring!
    O Most Still!

We deem it proper, meet, and right enough
    to speak to You

more or less directly—duly or not
    assuming some

interest on your part. We speak to You
    concerning much

You must already know. We often praise
    the majesty

of Your holiness, knowing next to naught
    of holiness;

of holiness we possess scant context.
    Regardless, we

dare to praise You for the sometime sweetness
    of the many

gifts apparently bestowed, and—despite
    our more common

habits of complaint—we praise You, giddy,
    and blinking still

at the intermittent, quiet, subtle,
    altogether

inexplicable pulse of joy rising,
    compensating

recurrent daily pain. We acknowledge
    that we should yet

exalt Your dear, capacious names, Your One
    and Holy Name.

We hasten yet to bless You, worship You,
    offer meager

thanks to You, and glorify You, the God
      Who is, Who is,

Who alone occasions life, insofar
      as we can say.

We apprehend with contrite heart, humble
      spirit, that we

should pledge to You our will, our wits, our breath,
      for it is You

Who have thus far deigned to bestow on us
      some little bit

of truth. Who among us can speak of all
      Your mighty works

or of your silence? Who make Your praises
      heard? Who can tell

of the odd miracle at sundry times
      or Your famous

disinclination to meddle in ways
      detectable?

O Master of All, of heaven and earth
      and of all dim

created beings, both the apparent
      and undisclosed,

You sit upon the throne of glory, look
      upon all depths.

You are invisible, unknowable,
      ineffable,

without beginning, without change,
      Fathering our

Lord Jesus Christ, our God, our Savior, Whom
      we call our Hope,

Who—in Himself—reveals You, our Maker.
      In Himself, He

proves the living, Unwritten Word, true God,
      Wisdom before

time, through Whom has come the Holy Spirit
      to be revealed,

which Spirit remains the Spirit of Truth,
     the Gift of our

late, filial adoption, pledge of an
     inheritance

yet to arrive. Despite our grim, our gloom,
     remember us.

Nepsis [Νήψις]

Notice how the piercing winter chill fails quite
     to enter the heart's bright furnace.
O brilliant, bright furnace!

Notice how the yammering electorate also
     fails to obtain against the heart's quiet
any ground, any likely purchase
     to nudge the weight of long-acquired stillness.
O pulsing stillness!

What heat, what light, what pulse is this?

What recourse has the weary pilgrim save
     to stand before that endless beckoning,
     to draw his every scattered member into one,
     to draw, and so be drawn?

What shall he say?

O Braided Being, include within your deep enormity
     this, these, every, all.

Acknowledgments

The American Poetry Journal	"Exhumation" and "Matter of Translation"
Books & Culture	"Anaphora on Orcas Island" and "Nepsis"
Curator	"My God and My Dog"
Image	"Sweet Life," "Tempest," and "Adiáphora"
Letters Journal	"Of Late, Our Climate," "Archaeology: A Late Lecture," "Honor," "Beyond Knowing,"and "Ειρήνη"
Locomotive	"Erato at 61"
McMaster Journal of Theology and Ministry	"Slow Pilgrim"
The Paraclete Poetry Anthology, 2005–2016	"Subtle Sin," "Daily Sacrifice," "Late Sayings," "Recreation" and "Late Metanoia" (previously published as "Feed My Sheep"; "Recreation" also appeared as lyric in Alana Levanoski's composition *Christ Hymn*)

Plume	"Babel's Artifacts"
Post Road	"Forsaken and Foregone"
Poems for Ephesians, Wipf & Stock	"Epistle to the Ostensible Church"
What Did Jesus Ask: *Christian Leaders* *Reflect on His Questions* *of Faith*, Time Books	"Which Cup? What Baptism?"

About the Author

Librettist, essayist, translator, and author of nine poetry collections, Scott Cairns is Professor of English and Director of the Low-Residency MFA Program at Seattle Pacific University. His poems and essays have appeared in *Poetry*, *Image*, *Paris Review*, *The Atlantic Monthly*, and *The New Republic*, and both have been anthologized in multiple editions of *Best American Spiritual Writing*. He blogs for the Religion Section of *The Huffington Post*. His recent books include *Slow Pilgrim: The Collected Poems* (2015), *Idiot Psalms* (2014), *Endless Life* (translations and adaptations of Christian mystics, 2014), and a book-length essay, *The End of Suffering* (2009). His spiritual memoir, *Short Trip to the Edge*, recently has been translated into Greek and Romanian. He received a Guggenheim Fellowship in 2006 and the Denise Levertov Award in 2014. His new projects include *Descent to the Heart*, verse adaptations of selections from the writings of Saint Isaak of Syria, and a new poetry collection, *Late Testament*.

About Paraclete Press

Who We Are

As the publishing arm of the Community of Jesus, Paraclete Press presents a full expression of Christian belief and practice—from Catholic to Evangelical, from Protestant to Orthodox, reflecting the ecumenical charism of the Community and its dedication to sacred music, the fine arts, and the written word. We publish books, recordings, sheet music, and video/DVDs that nourish the vibrant life of the church and its people.

What We Are Doing

Books

PARACLETE PRESS BOOKS show the richness and depth of what it means to be Christian. While Benedictine spirituality is at the heart of who we are and all that we do, our books reflect the Christian experience across many cultures, time periods, and houses of worship.

We have many series, including *Paraclete Essentials*; *Paraclete Fiction*; *Paraclete Poetry*; *Paraclete Giants*; and for children and adults, *All God's Creatures*, books about animals and faith; and *San Damiano Books*, focusing on Franciscan spirituality. Others include *Voices from the Monastery* (men and women monastics writing about living a spiritual life today), *Active Prayer*, and new for young readers: *The Pope's Cat*. We also specialize in gift books for children on the occasions of Baptism and First Communion, as well as other important times in a child's life, and books that bring creativity and liveliness to any adult spiritual life.

The MOUNT TABOR BOOKS series focuses on the arts and literature as well as liturgical worship and spirituality; it was created in conjunction with the Mount Tabor Ecumenical Centre for Art and Spirituality in Barga, Italy.

Music

The PARACLETE RECORDINGS label represents the internationally acclaimed choir *Gloriæ Dei Cantores*, the *Gloriæ Dei Cantores Schola*, and the other instrumental artists of the *Arts Empowering Life Foundation*.

Paraclete Press is the exclusive North American distributor for the Gregorian chant recordings from St. Peter's Abbey in Solesmes, France. Paraclete also carries all of the Solesmes chant publications for Mass and the Divine Office, as well as their academic research publications.

In addition, PARACLETE PRESS SHEET MUSIC publishes the work of today's finest composers of sacred choral music, annually reviewing over 1,000 works and releasing between 40 and 60 works for both choir and organ.

Video

Our video/DVDs offer spiritual help, healing, and biblical guidance for a broad range of life issues including grief and loss, marriage, forgiveness, facing death, understanding suicide, bullying, addictions, Alzheimer's, and Christian formation.

Learn more about us at our website: www.paracletepress.com or phone us toll-free at 1.800.451.5006

SCAN
TO
READ
MORE

You may also be interested in these collections
by Scott Cairns . . .

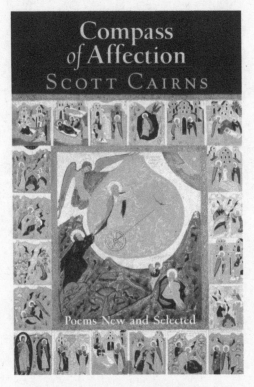

Compass of Affection
New and Selected Poems

ISBN 978-1-55725-503-7 | $25, Hardcover

"Cairns seeks compassionate ways to apply the lessons of
theologians or of Christ to his own life;
one does not need to be Christian, or even religious, to
profit from what he finds." —*Publishers Weekly*

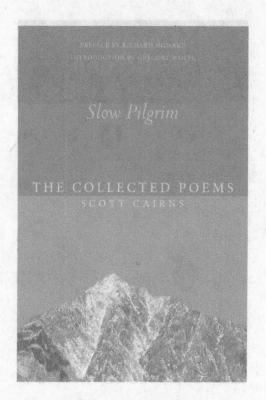

Slow Pilgrim
The Collected Poems

ISBN 978-1-61261-657-5 | $39, Trade paper

"Cairns' poetry draws us to direct our thoughts above the
everyday and consider the gratuity, the simple givenness, of
creation and because of this, to return to the everyday with
trembling reverence." —*Englewood Review of Books*

Endless Life
Poems of the Mystics

ISBN 978-1-61261-520-2 | $18, Trade paper

"Anyone attending this collection will be introduced to a multitude . . . bearing common witness to the relentless and ecstatic love of God and the real possibility of our participation in it." —*Eighth Day Books*

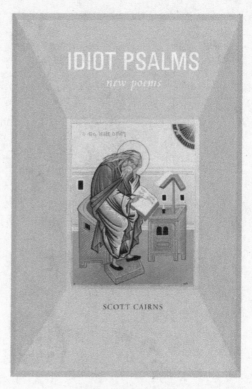

Idiot Psalms
New Poems

ISBN 978-1-61261-515-8 | $17, Trade paper

"Scott Cairns is perhaps the most important and promising religious poet of his generation."—*Prairie Schooner*

Available at bookstores
Paraclete Press | 1-800-451-5006
www.paracletepress.com